That's
Wild!
TM

Creepy Centipedes

by Patrick Merrick

Sundance/Newbridge Educational Publishing, LLC
One Beeman Road
P.O. Box 740
Northborough, MA 01532-0740
800-343-8204
www.sundancepub.com

Adapted from *Naturebooks,* published in 2003 by The Child's World®, Inc.
P.O. Box 326
Chanhassen, MN 55317-0326

Photo Credits: Front cover © Gerold and Cynthia Merker/Visuals Unlimited;
pp. 2, 22 © Robert and Linda Mitchell; p. 6 © Brian Kenney; p. 9 © B. Borrell
Casals, Frank Lane Picture Agency/Corbis; p. 10 © George Grall/National
Geographic; p. 13 © Raymond A. Mendez/Animals Animals; pp. 14, 21
© Michael and Patricia Fogden/Corbis; p. 17 © Paul Freed/Animals Animals;
p. 18 (top) © Carol Hughes, Gallo Images/Corbis; p. 25 © Steve Kaufman/
Corbis; p. 26 (top) © E. R. Degginger/Color-Pic; p. 26 (bottom) © Jack
Wilburn/Animals Animals; p. 29 © Donald Specker/Animals Animals; p. 30
© Art Wolfe/The Image Bank; back cover, p. 18 (bottom) © Zig Leszczynski/
Animals Animals

ISBN-13: 978-0-7608-9341-8
ISBN-10: 0-7608-9341-1

Printed in Canada

Contents

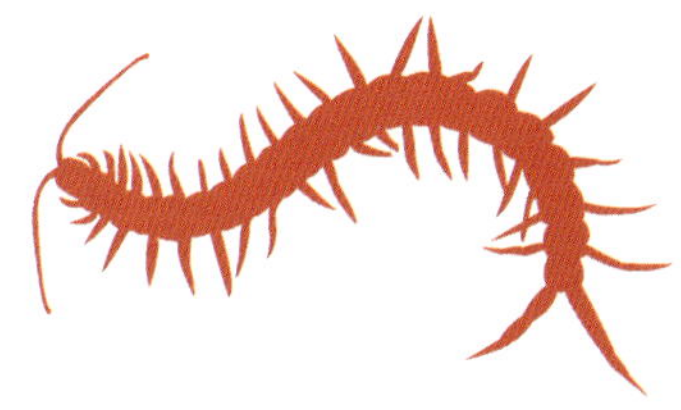

The summer is hot, but it's cool near the river.
You are watching the animals around you.
A bird **on a branch** is singing. You see
its two legs. A squirrel is climbing a tree. It
has four legs. A spider is spinning a web.
It has eight legs. Then you pick up a rock.
A small creature *scurries away.*
It has dozens of legs!

It's a centipede!

How many legs can you
count on this centipede?

Centipedes look **like insects,** but they are not. Insects have three body parts. Centipedes have two. Insects have six legs. Centipedes have a lot more legs than that! In fact, they seem to be more like **lobsters and shrimp.**

A centipede's body is made up of sections, or **segments.** Each segment has two legs—one leg on each side. Centipedes can have as few as 30 legs. Others can have more than **100 legs.** The word *centipede* means "hundred feet."

All centipedes have two body parts—the head and the body itself.

9

A centipede has **long feelers** on its head called **antennae.** Under its head are claws that are poisonous. It also has a **hard shell** that covers its body. This protects the centipede.

Centipedes are usually gray or reddish brown in color. They often grow to be about an inch long. But **some grow much longer.** The giant centipede of South America is the longest. It can grow to be more than 10 inches long!

The arrows are pointing at the black tips of this centipede's claws.

Centipedes are **predators.** They **hunt** and kill other animals for food. Most centipedes eat only insects. But larger centipedes also eat frogs, **mice,** and even snakes!

A centipede moves very fast to catch its food. It also makes use of its flat body as it looks for things to eat. It is able to **squeeze** into tight places. When it finds something, the centipede **grabs it** with its claws. Then the centipede shoots it full of poison and kills it.

This centipede has caught an insect for its meal.

Centipedes live in **warm places.** But they also need to live where they can get wet. If they are trapped inside of a dry house, they will **shrivel up** and die.

Usually centipedes stay outside. They look for dead plants or damp places to live. They can be found in **rotting wood,** under rocks, and in leaf piles. But sometimes they live in people's basements.

This large centipede lives in Malaysia.

A few kinds of centipedes **give birth** to live babies. But most centipedes lay eggs in dirt or rotting wood. The female lays many eggs at once. Then she **curls herself** around the eggs. This is how she protects them. From time to time, she cleans the eggs by licking them. After the **eggs hatch,** many mothers stay with their babies. They take care of them and try to protect them.

This giant centipede is guarding her eggs with her body.

17

Baby centipedes look like adult centipedes. But they have just a few body segments and a **couple of legs.** When the babies start to grow, they **molt,** or shed their skin. A new, bigger skin is waiting under the old one. The babies **molt many times.** Each time they do, they get more segments and more legs. A centipede can live for more than six years!

Top Photo: Young centipedes like these can be found in South Africa.

Bottom Photo: A giant centipede has just shed its skin.

Centipedes and millipedes are very different from each other. Centipedes are skinny and flat. Millipedes are **long and round.** Their shell is also much harder than a centipede's shell.

Millipedes have four legs on each segment instead of two. Their **legs are shorter** than a centipede's legs. And they do not have poisonous claws.

Count this millipede's body segments and multiply by four. That's how many legs it has!

Even though millipedes have more legs, they are **slower** than centipedes. They can't get away from their enemies by running. So they find other ways to stay safe. Often, they curl up into a **tight ball.** Their hard shell can protect them. They also have openings on the sides of their body. These openings let out liquids that **smell and taste bad.** Enemies quickly change their mind about trying to eat the millipede!

This millipede has rolled its body into a ball to protect itself.

Millipedes are **not hunters** like centipedes are. Instead, they are **scavengers.** They eat plants and insects that are dead and **decaying.** Sometimes millipedes dig for this rotting food in leaf piles and **garbage.** They also eat the roots and leaves of young plants.

This rain forest millipede is crawling over a decaying leaf.

8 Do Centipedes Have Enemies?

A lot of animals, such as frogs, birds, and rodents, eat centipedes. So centipedes must protect themselves. Usually they just hide or **run away** from their enemies. But if they are trapped, they might **attack** with their claws. The poison from them can kill small animals. But it is not deadly to people.

Others can try something else. They break off their legs! The legs **wiggle** and distract the enemy. Meanwhile, the centipede runs away.

Top Photo: This desert centipede is scurrying under a rock.

Bottom Photo: This soil centipede isn't safe out in the open.

Centipedes are not very dangerous. Some people even keep **large ones as pets.** But most people think of centipedes as pests. They **get into homes** and hide in corners, boxes, and shoes. It might seem like they help out around the house by eating lots of insects. But people don't want to be **startled** by a centipede. And they certainly don't want to be bitten by one!

Centipedes like this one can be found in people's homes.

Centipedes seem **strange** to most people. They might even scare others. But no matter how weird or frightening they may look, centipedes are an **important** part of our world!

Here you can see just the head, antennae, and legs of a centipede in Peru.

Glossary

antennae long feelers on the head of some creatures that are used to sense objects

decaying rotting

molt to shed the outer layer of skin, fur, or feathers

predators animals that hunt and kill other animals for food

scavengers animals that eat trash or decaying plants and animals

segments separate parts that when put together make up something larger

Index